Jackie Robinson

Jennifer Strand

abdopublishing.com

Published by Abdo Zoom™, PO Box 398166, Minneapolis, Minnesota 55439. Copyright © 2017 by Abdo Consulting Group, Inc. International copyrights reserved in all countries. No part of this book may be reproduced in any form without written permission from the publisher. Abdo Zoom™ is a trademark and logo of Abdo Consulting Group, Inc.

Printed in the United States of America, North Mankato, Minnesota
072016
092016

Cover Photo: DG/AP Images,
Interior Photos: DG/AP Images, 1; Hulton Archive/Getty Images, 5, 17; David Sucsy/iStockphoto, 6; AP images, 7, 8, 10, 11, 12, 14–15, 16, 18; J. R. Eyerman/The LIFE Picture Collection/Getty Images, 9; Keystone/Getty Images, 13; JW/AP Images, 19

Editor: Emily Temple
Series Designer: Madeline Berger
Art Direction: Dorothy Toth

Publisher's Cataloging-in-Publication Data
Names: Strand, Jennifer, author.
Title: Jackie Robinson / by Jennifer Strand.
Description: Minneapolis, MN : Abdo Zoom, [2017] | Series: Trailblazing athletes
    | Includes bibliographical references and index.
Identifiers: LCCN 2016941527 | ISBN 9781680792515 (lib. bdg.) |
    ISBN 9781680794199 (ebook) | 9781680795080 (Read-to-me ebook)
Subjects: LCSH: Robinson, Jackie, 1919-1972--Juvenile literature. | Baseball
    Players--United States--Biography--Juvenile literature. | African American
    baseball players--Juvenile literature.
Classification: DDC 796.357092 [B]--dc23
LC record available at http://lccn.loc.gov/2016941527

Table of Contents

Introduction

Jackie Robinson made history.
Major League Baseball did
not allow black players.
In 1947 he became the first.

Early Life

Jackie was born on
January 31, 1919.
He grew up in California.

Jackie was good at sports.
He played four sports in college.

Robinson was a baseball star.

CANCELLED
IN ACCORDANCE WITH
CITY ORDINANCE № 1172
RELATING TO PROHIBITION
OF SPORTS EVENTS BETWEEN
WHITE and COLORED

But the United States was segregated. Blacks did not have the same rights as whites. Even Major League Baseball teams refused black players.

Robinson joined the
Kansas City Monarchs.

They were an all-black
baseball team. He played well.

The Brooklyn Dodgers decided to sign Robinson.

They were a major league team.
Some people were mad.
Robinson dealt with **racism**.

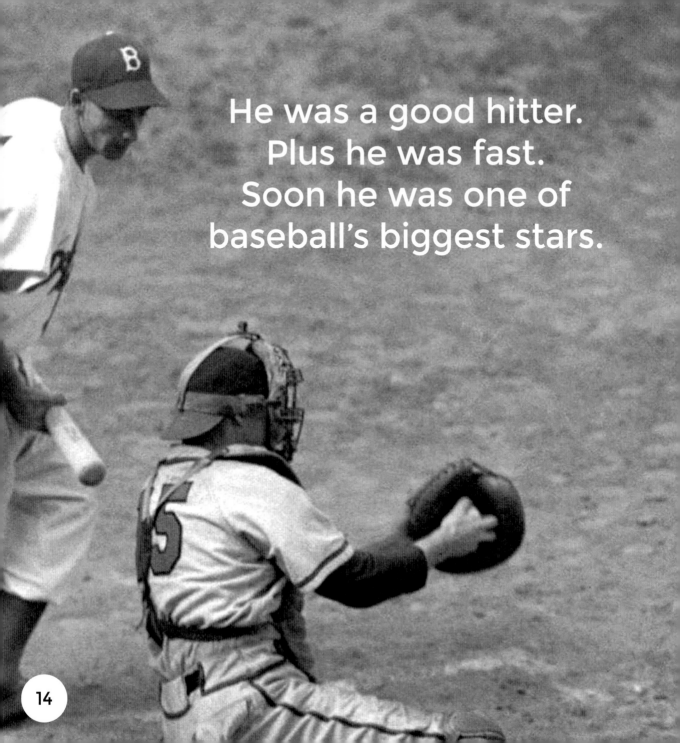

He was a good hitter.
Plus he was fast.
Soon he was one of
baseball's biggest stars.

Legacy

Robinson changed people's opinions.

He showed black players belonged in Major League Baseball. This helped integrate the United States.

Robinson played 10 seasons. After baseball Robinson still worked for change.

He died on October 24, 1972.

Jackie Robinson

Born: January 31, 1919

Birthplace: Cairo, Georgia

Sport: Baseball

Known For: Robinson became the first black baseball player to play in the major leagues since the 1800s.

Died: October 24, 1972

1919: Jack Roosevelt Robinson is born on January 31.

1944: Robinson plays for the all-black Kansas City Monarchs.

1947: Robinson becomes the first black player in Major League Baseball since the 1800s.

1957: Robinson retires from baseball.

1962: Robinson is the first African American inducted into the National Baseball Hall of Fame.

1972: Robinson dies on October 24.

Glossary

integrate – to bring groups of people together.

racism – treating someone poorly or taking away their rights because of the color of their skin.

rights – things that people can do under the law.

segregated – when a group of people is separated from others, often in a way that is unfair.

Booklinks

For more information
on Jackie Robinson, please visit
booklinks.abdopublishing.com

Zoom™ In on Biographies!

Learn even more with the Abdo Zoom
Biographies database. Check out
abdozoom.com for more information.

Index